Copyright 2020 - by Beth Costanzo

TRACING PRACTICE

EASTER BUNNY

EGGS EGGS

CHOCOLATE

CHICKEN CHICKEN

SPRING SPRING

WWW.ADVENTURESOFSCUBAJACK.COM

Draw a line to connect the matching Easter pictures.

WWW.ADVENTURESOFSCUBAJACK.COM

EASTER COUNTING

Count the Easter pictures in each row. Write how many you counted on the line at the end of the row.

_____

🐰🐰🐰🐰🐰 _____

🧺🧺 _____

🐤🐤🐤🐤🐤🐤🐤 _____

🐰🐰🐰🐰🐰🐰🐰🐰🐰 _____

🧺🧺🧺🧺🧺🧺 _____

🐤 _____

🐰🐰🐰 _____

🧺🧺🧺🧺🧺🧺🧺🧺🧺🧺 _____

🐤🐤🐤🐤 _____

🐰🐰🐰🐰🐰🐰🐰🐰🐰 _____

WWW.ADVENTURESOFSCUBAJACK.COM

WHAT COMES NEXT?

Look at the pictures on each line and study the pattern they are in. If you continued the pattern, what picture would come next? Cut out the correct picture from the next page and glue it at the end of the correct line.

BUNNY CRAFT

After coloring in the bunny and eggs, ask a grown-up to help cut out and fold them plus tape the tail on the bunny

WWW.ADVENTURESOFSCUBAJACK.COM

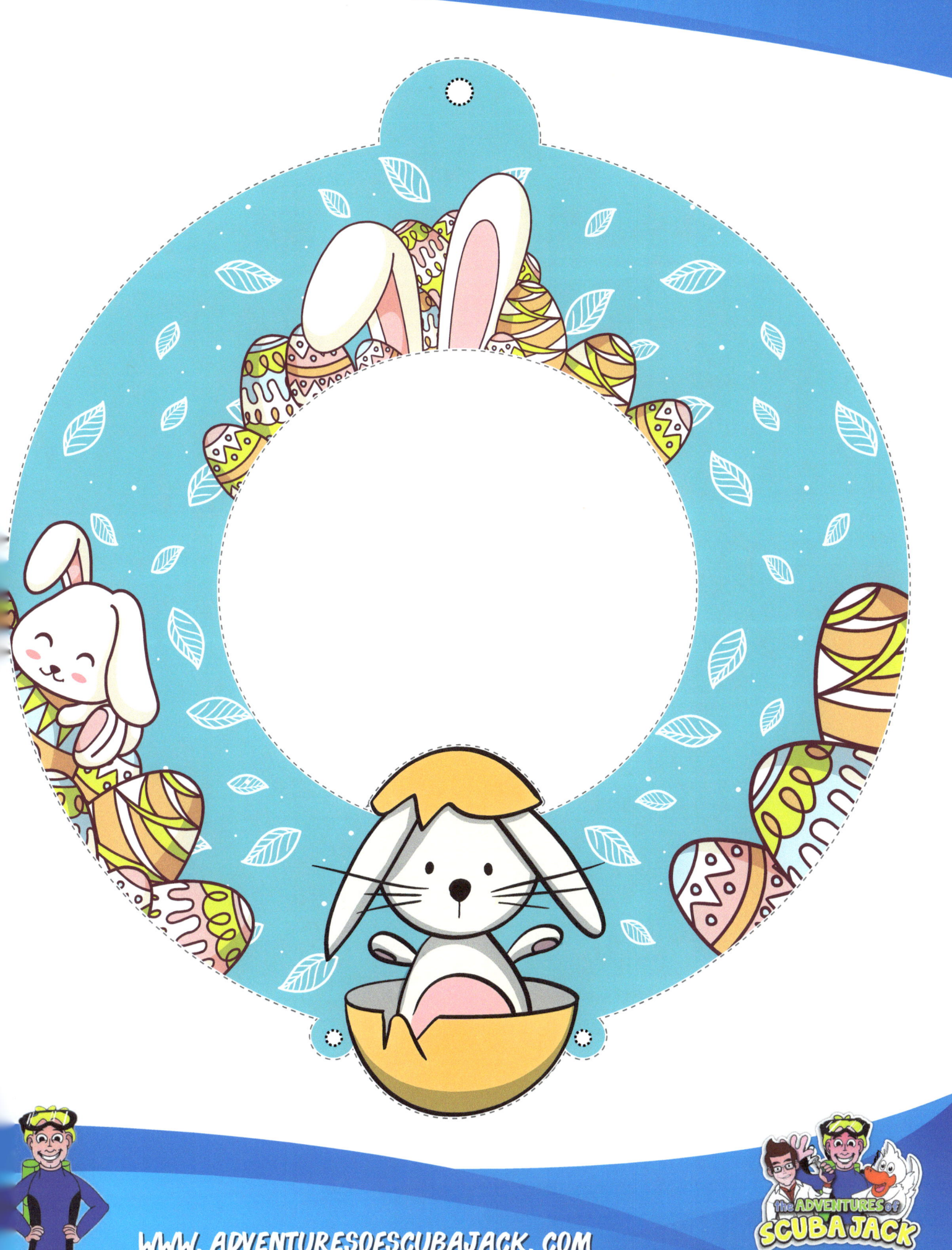

It'll look like this:

WWW.ADVENTURESOFSCUBAJACK.COM

Crumple up little balls of yellow tissue paper and glue them on the Easter chick.

www.adventuresofscubajack.com

Glue little balls of white tissue, cotton balls or pieces of popcorn on this Easter lamb.

WWW.ADVENTURESOFSCUBAJACK.COM

Fill the basket with Easter Eggs. You can use the eggs on the next page or make your own!

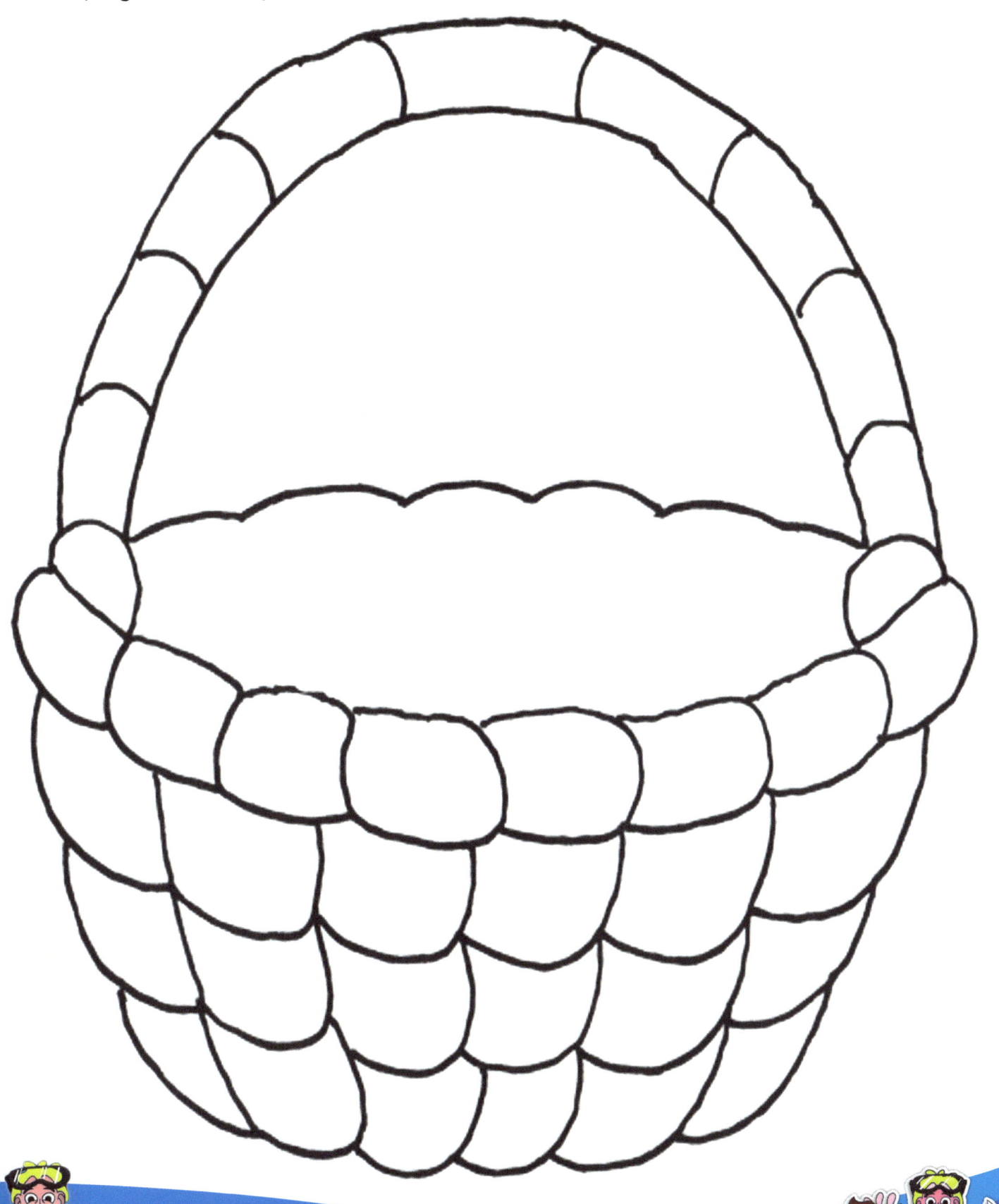

WWW.ADVENTURESOFSCUBAJACK.COM

Cut along the puzzle lines and then try to put the Easter Bunny back together.

WWW.ADVENTURESOFSCUBAJACK.COM

COLORING PAGE

www. adventuresofscubajack. com

COLORING PAGE

WWW.ADVENTURESOFSCUBAJACK.COM

ROLL AND GRAPH

Make our Easter Box Project to create a die that you can roll and use to fill in this graph. Each time you roll, fill in a box on the graph above the picture that you rolled.

6						
5						
4						
3						
2						
1						

Draw a circle around the picture that you rolled the most.

Draw a square around the picture that you rolled the least.

WWW.ADVENTURESOFSCUBAJACK.COM

Cut out the box pattern below.
Fold along each line so that pictures are on the outside.
Place glue on the flaps one at a time and form the box.

www.ingramcontent.com/pod-product-compliance
Lightning Source LLC
Chambersburg PA
CBHW041438010526
44118CB00002B/116